COTTON
Now & Then

Fabric-Making from Boll to Bolt

Dedicated to all our cotton-pickin' kids:

> *Jordan, Jonathan, Shayna, and Marni Willing;*
> *Abigail Dock;*
> *and Elijah, Isaac, and baby Alice Morse.*

QUILT CREDITS:

> Photographs by Charles White
> Page 2: Sampler by Karen Willing
> Kaleidoscope by Linda Richardson Goines
> Page 5: Bow Tie by Karen Willing
> Page 7: Ohio Star by Karen Willing

The photographs of modern cotton processing have been supplied by the National Cotton Council, and are reprinted from *Cotton: Field to Fabric in Forty Frames*, with the exception of the photograph on page 25 which was supplied by Cotton Incorporated. We would like to express our sincere appreciation to both organizations for their encouragement and support.

ISBN 0-9641820-2-5 (hardback)
ISBN 0-9641820-3-3 (paperback)

Production and Design Assistance: Robin Weisz

Printed in Hong Kong by Regent Publishing Services Ltd.

For additional copies, or for *Quilting Now & Then*, send $12.95 for each hardback or $8.95 for each paperback plus $3.00 postage and handling to:

Now & Then Publications
725 Beach Street
Ashland, OR 97520
FAX: 541-482-7937

COTTON
Now & Then

Fabric-Making from Boll to Bolt

Written by

Karen Bates Willing
and Julie Bates Dock

Illustrated by

Sarah Morse

Now & Then Publications 🌸 725 Beach Street 🌸 Ashland, OR 97520

A fabric store's a wonderland for every mom and child,
For everyone loves colors and the patterns bright and wild.

Today the Johnson clan is shopping at their favorite store.
Mom wants to buy some yardage, but the kids want to explore.

While Shirley chooses what she needs her daughter Sue stands by,
But not so Hank and brother Fred: the fabric's caught their eye.

Now, Shirley Johnson is a mom who sews both night and day.
The kind of sewing that she does is quilting, by the way.

Her grandma taught her how to quilt: the lesson's not forgotten.
And when she buys her fabric she makes sure it's made of cotton.

She puts the cloth upon her shelves, arranging it just so.
The kids admire what Mom bought. She'll make great quilts, they know.

Today Sue asks a question that's been going through her head:
"Where does the fabric come from for the quilt that's on my bed?"

Then Fred says, "Don't be silly, we just bought it at the store."
"I know that," Sue says patiently, "but I mean something more.

"Where does it come from at the start? From bushes, plants or trees?
I want to know how fabric's made. Oh, won't you tell us, please?"

"Silk comes from worms," says Shirley, "fluffy sheep provide our wool,
While manmade cloth like rayon sure helps keep our closets full.

"But cotton's what I know the best, so I will tell you how
They made it in great-grandma's day and how they make it now.

"It starts with one small cotton seed, that's planted in the ground.
It needs a lot of nice, rich soil to keep it safe and sound.

"It needs at least two hundred days without a frost or snow.
That's why it's found in Southern states, a nice warm place to grow."

Fred wants to know "When's planting time?" "It's March or April, dear,"
Says Shirley, adding that by June new blossoms will appear.

"But as the plant is growing tall, so too are all the weeds.
They try to take the nutrients the cotton really needs."

"Wait, Mommy, what are nutrients?" "Well, Hank, now let me think.
I guess I'd say they're vitamins and minerals, like zinc.

"The early cotton farmers had no pesticides, you know,
So they relied on geese to eat the weeds along each row."

"But didn't geese eat cotton, too?" says little Hank, concerned.
"Oh no, the taste of cotton plants was terrible, they learned.

"As blossoms slowly turn to pink, then reddish purple, too,
The petals will begin to fall. A seed pod soon pokes through.

"The seed pod will begin to grow to form a *cotton boll*.
This is the part bugs love to eat: boll weevils take their toll."

"A weevil? What a funny word! What can it be?" asks Fred.
"It's a nasty little insect that the cotton farmers dread.

10

"In August cotton bolls will burst. They open one by one,
Which makes it very difficult to get the picking done.

"The workers had to harvest many times in olden days.
They picked each boll before the weevils gobbled it away.

"Today insecticides control the weevil population.
And big machines are used to help improve the situation.

"The farmer waits till all the bolls burst fibers white and new.
He uses his machine to harvest once, and then he's through.

"Now after all the cotton's picked it's time to clean within.
To pull out seeds and dirt and leaves we use the *cotton gin*.

"We should thank Eli Whitney for he built the cotton gin.
Its rows of teeth turn round and round. Boy, you should see them spin.

"Before the gin, the people had to pull seeds one by one.
With Eli Whitney's cotton gin the work is quickly done.

"The seeds aren't thrown away—oh no! They still have work to do.
They help make soap and cooking oil and fertilizer too.

"Now once the cotton's nice and clean it's pressed into a *bale*,
A block that weighs 500 pounds. At last it is for sale.

"The bales go to a factory that's called a *textile mill*.
Our cotton now gets pulled and stretched and yanked and tugged
                . . . until

"The pieces are all thin and straight and lined up in a row.
This process is called *carding* and it started long ago."

"It's just like when your hair's a mess and tangled up," says Sue.
"Mom combs it to get out the knots. The cotton's combed like you!"

"But carding cotton, unlike hair, is harder and takes longer.
If workers make the fibers straight, the fabric will be stronger.

"In times long past, they combed by hand and it was slow indeed.
Today we have machines that card the cotton with great speed.

"The next step is the *spinning* where the fiber's turned to thread."
"Like spinning wheels I've read about in fairy tales?" asks Fred.

"That's right," says Shirley. "Spinning wheels twist fibers round and round,
To make a thread that's strong and light, and then on spools it's wound.

"The spinning wheel Rapunzel used worked well for small amounts,
But in our modern times we need production—that's what counts.

"So factories use huge machines to manufacture thread.
The process is the same, although the old ways are not dead.

"Some people still use spinning wheels, I'm very glad to say.
They help preserve our heritage by doing it this way.

"What happens once we have the thread?" the kids all want to know,
"It doesn't seem like fabric yet. The process seems so slow."

"The thread now goes to a machine that weaves it—called a *loom*.
Here threads are criss-crossed up and down. They will be fabric soon."

"Oh, I've done that," says Sue, "by weaving ribbons in and out.
Go over, then go under—that's what weaving's all about."

"The looms we use today are like the looms of times long past.
The thread's still woven as you did. The fabric's here at last.

"But mommy, that seems awfully dull. It just looks plain old white!"
"Yes, Hank, the cotton's dyed to give us colors nice and bright."

"Our ancestors would dye their thread, then put it on the loom,
Or else they dyed the fabric, which took up a lot more room."

"You mean like dyeing Easter eggs?" the kids ask Shirley now.
"Yes, fabric's dunked in pots called *vats*—the pioneers knew how.

"They found that nuts and flowers could provide them with their dyes.
They stirred the cloth and watched as fabric changed before their eyes.

"Although we now make different dyes the process has not changed.
No matter how the dyeing's done, we get a color range.

"But if the fabric's all one color that gets awfully plain.
And so we have designs and prints that rarely are the same.

"Like flowers, stripes, and polka dots, and curlicues, and fish,
Like animals and stars and kites: whatever you may wish!

"The early printers carved designs on wood blocks. It was hard
To ink the blocks and press them on the fabrics yard by yard.

"To print with blocks takes lots of time, though it's still done today.
But fabric manufacturers have found a quicker way.

"Two hundred years ago there was a man named Thomas Bill
Who invented *roller printing*, and we use that process still.

"A roller puts the pattern on the fabric moving past.
Compared to blocks, the printing's now five hundred times as fast.

"And when the fabric has been dried, there's only one thing more:
It's wrapped on cardboard as a *bolt* and shipped off to the store."

As Shirley closes up the book, she says, "I never thought
It took so many folks to make the fabric that I bought!

"They work in fields and factories until the fabric's done.
Of all the jobs we've learned about which is your favorite one?"

Fred likes the weaving most of all, Sue likes the printer's art.
But little Hank says, "No, you guys! The geese are the best part!"

The Johnson kids have made their choice and now it's up to you:
If you were asked to pick a job, then which one would you do?